UFO Sightings

by Katie Chanez

CAPSTONE PRESS
a capstone imprint

Bright Idea Books are published by Capstone Press
1710 Roe Crest Drive, North Mankato, Minnesota 56003
www.mycapstone.com

Library of Congress Cataloging-in-Publication Data
Names: Chanez, Katie, author.
Title: UFO sightings / by Katie Chanez.
Description: North Mankato, Minnesota : Capstone Press, [2020] | Series: Aliens | Includes index.
Identifiers: LCCN 2018058401 (print) | LCCN 2018059082 (ebook) | ISBN
    9781543571172 (ebook) | ISBN 9781543571097 (hardcover) | ISBN 9781543574968 (pbk.)
Subjects: LCSH: Unidentified flying objects--Sightings and
    encounters--Juvenile literature.
Classification: LCC TL789.2 (ebook) | LCC TL789.2 .C43 2020 (print) | DDC 001.942--dc23
LC record available at https://lccn.loc.gov/2018058401

All internet sites appearing in back matter were available and accurate when this book was sent to press.

Editorial Credits
Editor: Claire Vanden Branden
Designer: Becky Daum
Production Specialist: Melissa Martin

Photo Credits
Alamy: Chronicle, 15; iStockphoto: apomares, 18–19, ElvisFontenot, 20–21, 28, gremlin, 16–17, ktsimage, 24–25, mscornelius, cover, oorka, 9, Sjo, 23, stevecoleimages, 31, tdub303, 6–7; North Wind Picture Archives: 10–11; Shutterstock Images: John D Sirlin, 26–27, Lori Martin, 12–13, Ursatii, 5

Design Elements: Shutterstock Images, Red Line Editorial

Printed in the United States of America.
PA70

TABLE OF CONTENTS

CHAPTER 1

IS THAT a UFO?

Kenneth Arnold was a pilot.

He was flying his plane one day in 1947.

He looked ahead. There was something

in the sky. Nine bright lights were flying

in a "V" shape. Were they army planes?

Or something else?

No one knows for sure. The lights were **unidentified flying objects** (UFOs). It was one of the first UFO reports.

UFOs are also called flying saucers. This is because some look like saucers skipping across the sky.

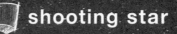 shooting star

Shooting stars are
often falling meteors.
From Earth they can
look like spaceships.

Most UFOs can be explained. Some are shooting stars. They can be airplanes or balloons. Others are just tricks on the eyes.

Sometimes people cannot find a reason for the objects. Some people say they are **alien** spaceships.

CHAPTER 2

HISTORY

People have reported strange flying objects for years. But "UFO" was not used until the 1950s.

People learned going to space was possible. Some people wondered. Could aliens travel to Earth?

Throughout history many people have not been able to explain strange shapes they have seen in the sky.

People who studied
John Winthrop's diary
believed he had seen a
real alien spaceship.

EARLY SIGHTINGS

One of the first UFO reports took place in 1639. John Winthrop was governor of Massachusetts. He wrote about a flying light. Believers think he saw a spaceship.

FIVE YEARS LATER

Winthrop reported another sighting. In 1644 two strange lights were in the sky. Another light was seen again a week later. Unknown voices were even heard this time.

People reported a strange crash in 1897. An object landed in Aurora, Texas. A reporter said it was a spaceship. He wrote that an alien died. Most people say he made it up. Believers think the alien body is still there.

A small grave in Aurora marks where people think the alien's body is buried.

CHAPTER 3

REPORTS

Many sightings were reported after Kenneth Arnold's. The government wanted answers. The U.S. Air Force started Project Blue Book in 1947. It looked into the reports.

The project workers said most objects could be explained. But some said the government lied. Many reports were kept secret. Believers think that proves aliens have visited.

Men and women from the air force worked on Project Blue Book until 1969.

1947 SIGHTINGS

Harold Dahl saw something strange in June 1947. He said six objects were flying above him. They got closer. Suddenly weird pieces fell from the sky. Then the objects flew away.

Two men from the air force came. They looked into what happened. The men took some of the pieces. They said Dahl's story might be true. But on their way home their plane crashed. Both men died.

Harold Dahl said that the UFOs he saw were shaped like donuts.

Some people said the air force crashed the plane. They thought the government wanted to hide the truth. But the air force said it did not crash the plane. It also said Dahl's report was a lie.

Some people think the air force crashed the plane because the pilots were going to tell government secrets about the UFO.

Many people thought the government was lying about the crash in Roswell.

Another sighting happened later that year. Something crashed near Roswell, New Mexico. The government said it was a weather balloon. But many thought this was a lie.

Many years later the government told the truth. The object was part of a secret project. The government could not tell people at the time.

CHAPTER 4

SIGHTINGS Today

People still report UFOs today. In 2008 many people reported something in Texas. They saw strange lights in the sky. The lights moved unlike anything they had ever seen.

The government said it was army airplanes. But the people were not so sure.

Some army airplanes can fly so fast that people mistake them for UFOs.

It's easy to make fake photos of UFOs with a computer. This is why people have a hard time believing photos of UFOs are real.

Today there are fewer reports than in the past. Many UFO photos are fake. It is hard to believe in something without **proof**.

FEWER SIGHTINGS

UFO reports are down. But people still see strange things in the sky. California has the most reported UFO sightings in the United States.

In 2017 the SpaceX Falcon 9
rocket flew at superfast speeds.
Many people thought it was
a UFO. But scientists quickly
explained the truth.

Some people think it is a waste of time to study UFOs. Instead they work on proving aliens have visited Earth.

Some people say many UFOs are too strange. They cannot be from Earth. But scientists say there is an answer for everything.

GLOSSARY

alien
a creature not from Earth

proof
the facts showing that
something is true

unidentified flying object (UFO)
an unknown object in the sky

TRIVIA

1. On March 13, 1997, many people saw strange UFOs in Phoenix, Arizona. Several lights were in a "V" shape. The government said it was from a military plane. But people who saw the lights think it was something from out of this world.

2. In June 2018 there was a report of a UFO in South Carolina. It was actually a U.S. Army parachute team performing in a nearby festival.

3. The Mutual UFO Network (MUFON) tracks and investigates UFO sightings across the country. It receives hundreds of reports each month.

ACTIVITY

SEARCH FOR UFOS

Believers say unknown shapes or lights in the sky must be alien spaceships. Scientists disagree. They say there is always a simple explanation. Go outside when the weather is clear and watch the sky. You can use a telescope or binoculars if you would like. Is there anything you see that you don't understand? Write a description of what you see or take a picture. What about it could make someone think it was alien? What are some possible scientific explanations?

FURTHER RESOURCES

Want to know more about UFOs? Learn more here:

Hile, Lori. *Aliens and UFOs: Myth or Reality.* North Mankato, Minn.: Capstone Press, 2019.

McCollum, Sean. *Handbook to UFOs, Crop Circles, and Alien Encounters.* North Mankato, Minn.: Capstone Press, 2017.

UFO Research – Queensland: Everything You Need to Know About UFOs
http://uforq.asn.au/kids

**Curious about the science behind UFOs?
Check out this website:**

PBS Learning Material: Identifying Flying Objects
https://tpt.pbslearningmedia.org/resource/f0e60a9b-759e-45b2-801e-dc491e853246/identifying-flying-objects

INDEX